Alfred's Premier Piano Course

Gayle Kowalchyk • E. L. Lancaster

Correlated Standard Repertoire

Alfred's Premier Piano Course: Masterworks 3 includes standard repertoire from the four stylistic periods to reinforce concepts introduced in *Lesson 3*. Except for page 9, the pieces are in their original form and have not been adapted. Dynamics, phrasing, fingering, and pedal are editorial in some selections. The editors also have added titles to untitled pieces. *Celebration Boogie*, on pages 10–11, is an original piece by the editors. It is included to represent swing style.

The pieces in this book correlate page by page with the materials in *Lesson 3*. They should be assigned according to the instructions in the upper right corner of selected pages of this book. They also may be assigned as review material at any time after the student has passed the designated lesson book page. In these pieces, terms or symbols that have not been used in *Lesson 3* are defined in footnotes or parentheses.

A compact disc recording is included with this book. It can serve as a *performance* model or as a *practice* companion. See information about the CD on page 32.

Performance skills and musical understanding are enhanced through *Premier Performer* suggestions for most pieces. Students will enjoy performing these pieces for family and friends in a formal recital or on special occasions. See the List of Compositions on page 32.

Cover Design by Ted Engelbart
Interior Design by Tom Gerou
Music Engraving by Linda Lusk

ISBN-10: 0-7390-9339-8
ISBN-13: 978-0-7390-9339-9

Use with Alfred's Premier Piano Course,
Lesson Book 3, page 6

The Chase

CD 1/2

Cornelius Gurlitt (1820–1901)
Op. 117, No. 15

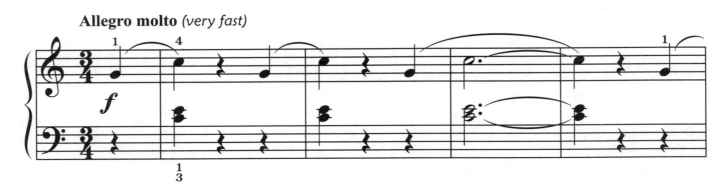

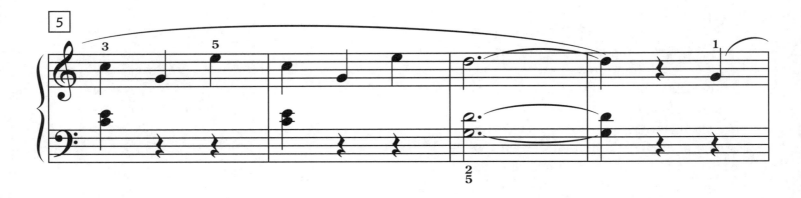

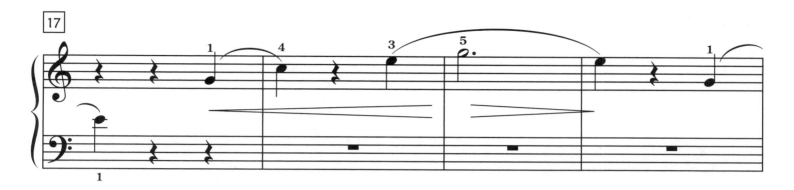

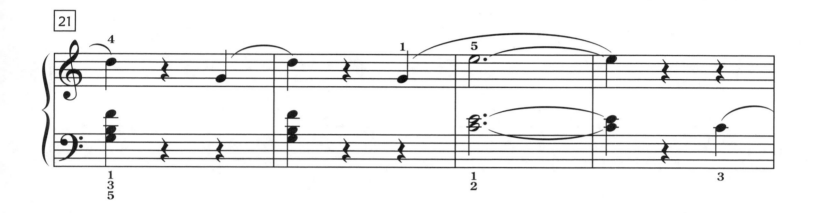

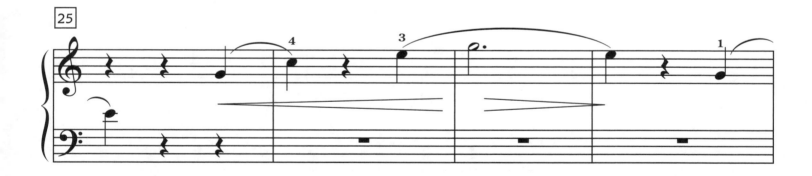

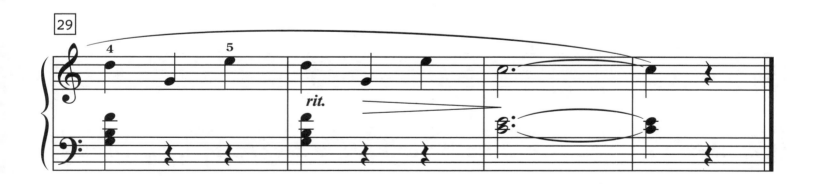

Premier Performer

When playing fast, feel the tempo as if each measure has just one beat.

Lesson Book: page 7

Bagatelle*

CD 3/4

Anton Diabelli
(1781–1858)

* *Bagatelle*, a French word meaning "trifle," is a short instrumental piece.

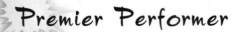

Premier Performer

*Listen carefully so that the LH chords
are softer than the RH melody.*

Soldier's March

CD 5/6

Louis Köhler
(1820–1886)

Premier Performer

Keep the tempo steady and emphasize the downbeat to create a march-like feel.

Écossaise* in G Major

CD 7/8

Franz Schubert (1797–1828)
D. 529, No. 3

*Both hands play
in treble clef.*

* An écossaise is an English country dance in $\frac{2}{4}$ meter
popular in the late 18th and early 19th centuries.

** *fz* (forzando) means "accented."

Little Dance

CD 9/10

Ludvig Schytte (1848–1909)
Op. 108, No. 1

Allegro moderato (*moderately fast*)

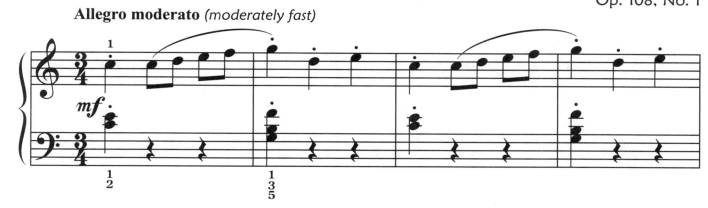

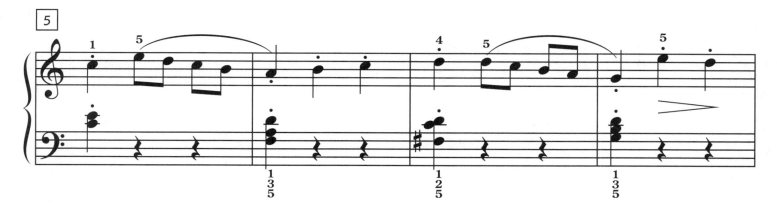

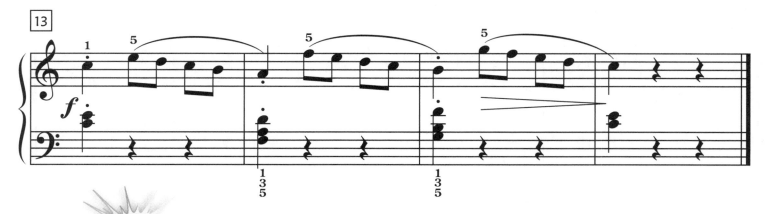

Premier Performer

Play the eighth notes with a slight crescendo to beat 1 of the next measure (except in measures 15–16).

Lesson Book: pages 14–15

Trumpet Fanfare

CD 11/12

Cornelius Gurlitt (1820–1901)
Op. 117, No. 8

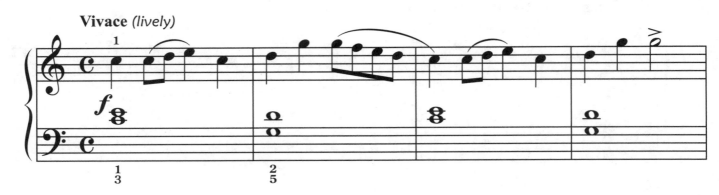

Premier Performer

Create a clear and bright melody by using strong RH fingers.

Jazzy Trumpets

CD 13/14

Cornelius Gurlitt (1820–1901)
Op. 117, No. 8
(adapted)

Premier Performer

This piece is an adaptation of Trumpet Fanfare using the ♩♩♩♩ rhythm pattern. For a longer performance, play the two pieces without stopping in between.

Lesson Book: pages 18–19

Celebration Boogie

(from *Boogie 'n' Blues, Book 2*)

CD 15/16

Gayle Kowalchyk
E. L. Lancaster

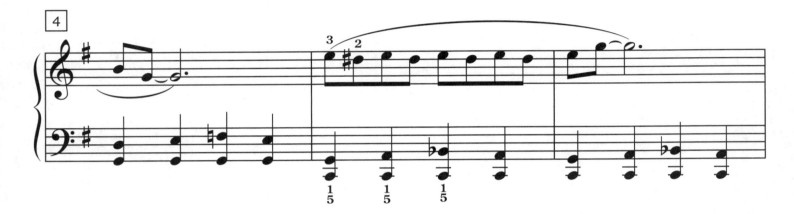

* Play the eighth notes a bit unevenly: long   short long   short

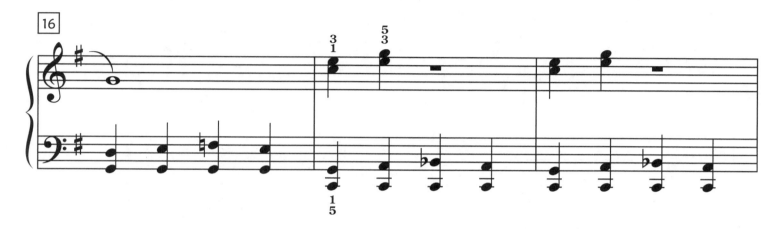

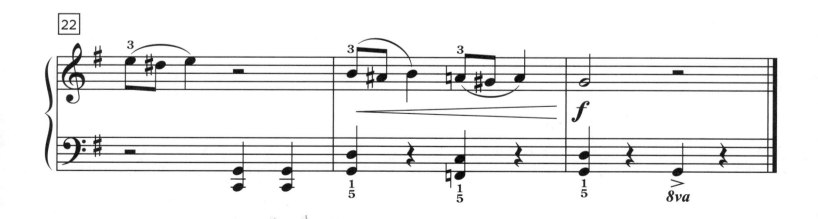

Premier Performer

Keep the tempo steady yet relaxed throughout the entire piece.

Lesson Book: pages 22–23

Song without Words

CD 17/18

Louis Köhler (1820–1886)
Op. 190, No. 27

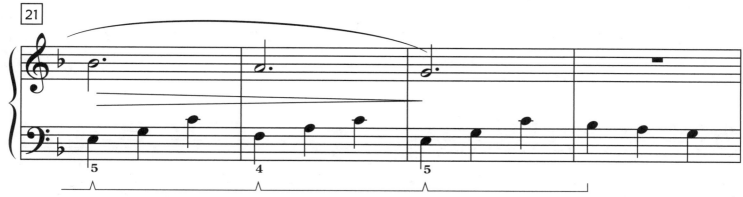

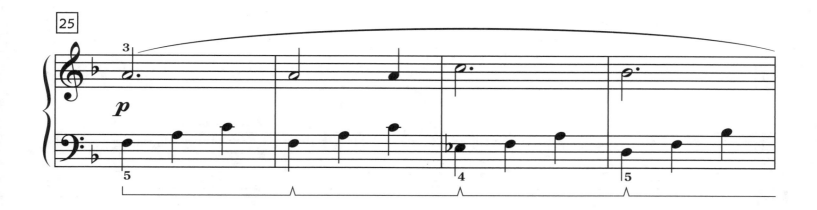

Premier Performer

Listen for smooth pedal changes with no gaps in sound.

Lesson Book: pages 24–25

Springtime Waltz

CD 19/20

Emil Breslaur (1836–1899)
Op. 46, No. 25

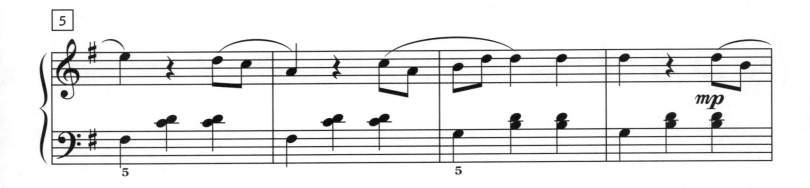

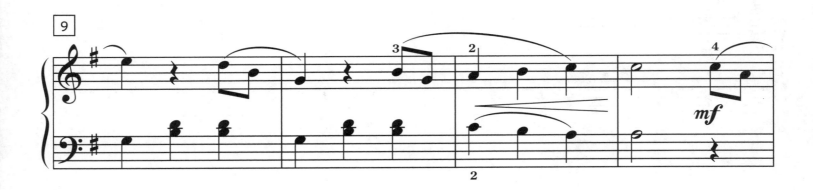

Premier Performer

Project the RH melody and play with a light touch to create an energetic mood.

Opening Act

CD 21/22

Ludvig Schytte (1848–1909)
Op. 108, No. 13

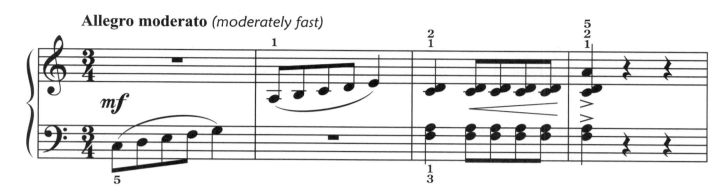

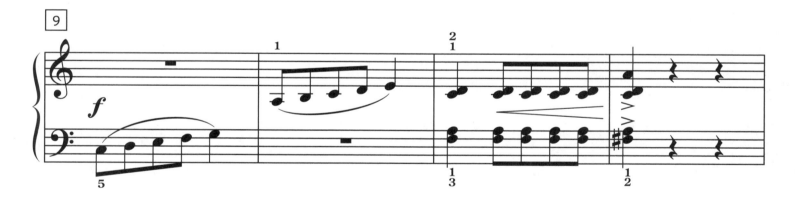

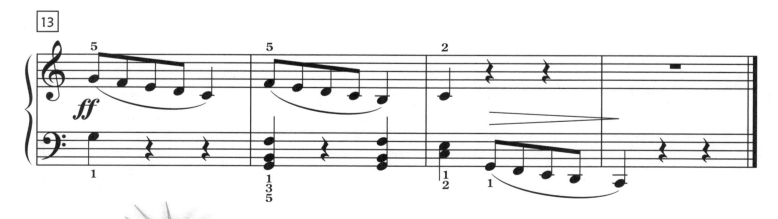

Premier Performer — *Choose a tempo that allows you to play moderately fast, with the repeated notes speaking clearly.*

Lesson Book: page 27

The Setting Sun

CD 23/24

Johann Christian Bach
(1735–1782)

* The short line (tenuto mark) means to play the note with
a slight emphasis and hold for its full rhythmic value.

Folk Dance

(from *For Children, Volume 1*)

CD 25/26

Béla Bartók (1881–1945)
Sz. 42, No. 6

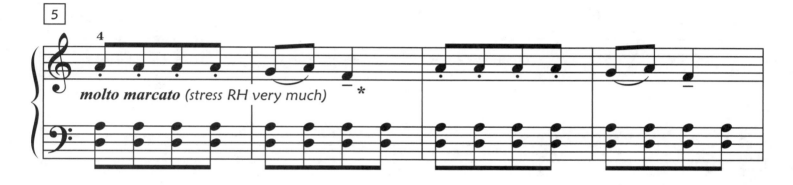

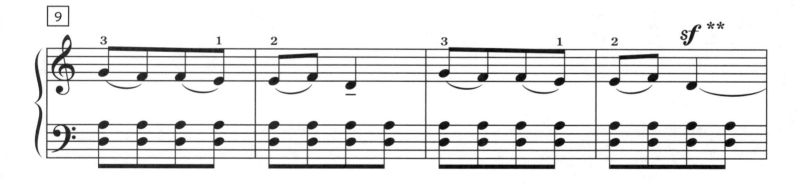

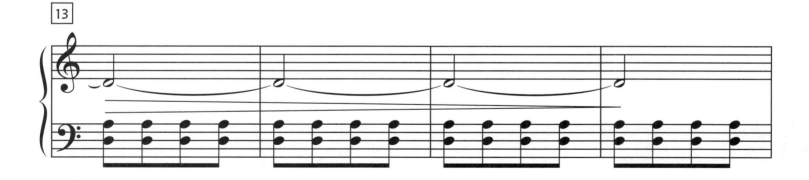

*The short line (tenuto mark) means to play the note with a slight emphasis and hold for its full rhythmic value.

** *sf* (sforzando) means "with a strong accent."

*The wedge accent means to play louder with a sharper attack than a regular accent.

una corda (Depress left pedal and hold to end of piece.)

* // (caesura) is a symbol that indicates a pause in the music.

The Bear

CD 27/28

Vladimir Rebikov
(1866–1920)

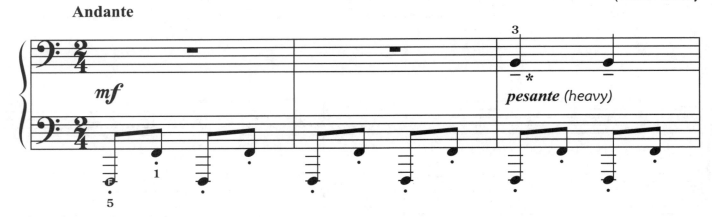

* The short line (tenuto mark) means to play the note with a slight emphasis
   and hold for its full rhythmic value.

Premier Performer

Paint a sound picture of a lumbering bear.
Use a steady LH and a strong RH.

* ![short stressed note symbol] means to play short, but stressed.

Lesson Book: page 35

Waltz in C Major

CD 29/30

Anton Diabelli
(1781–1858)

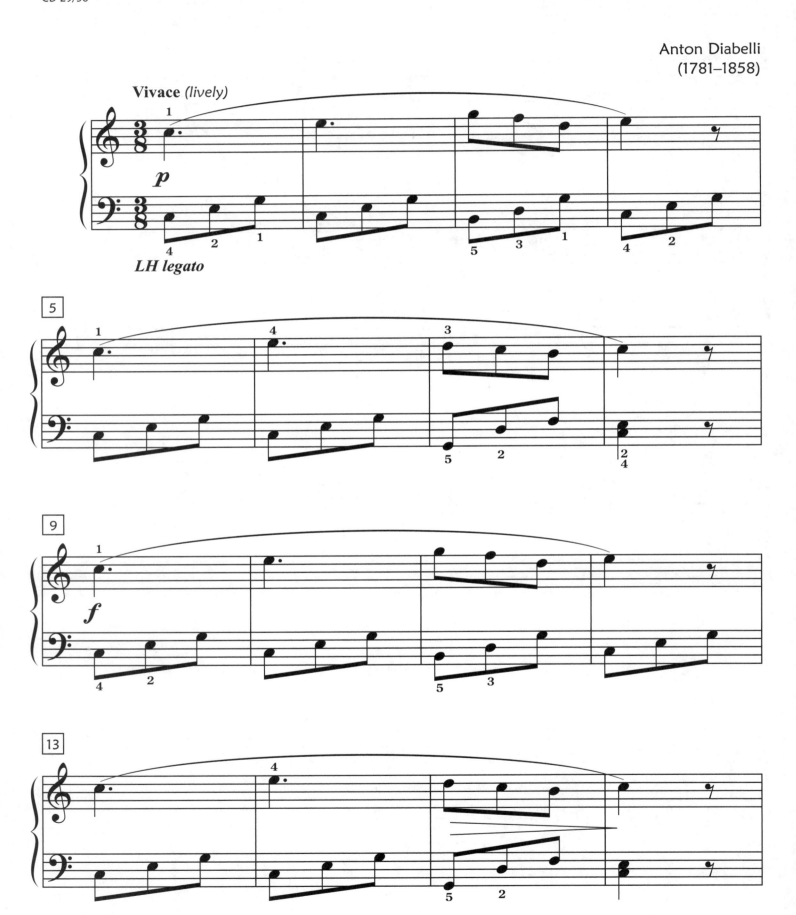

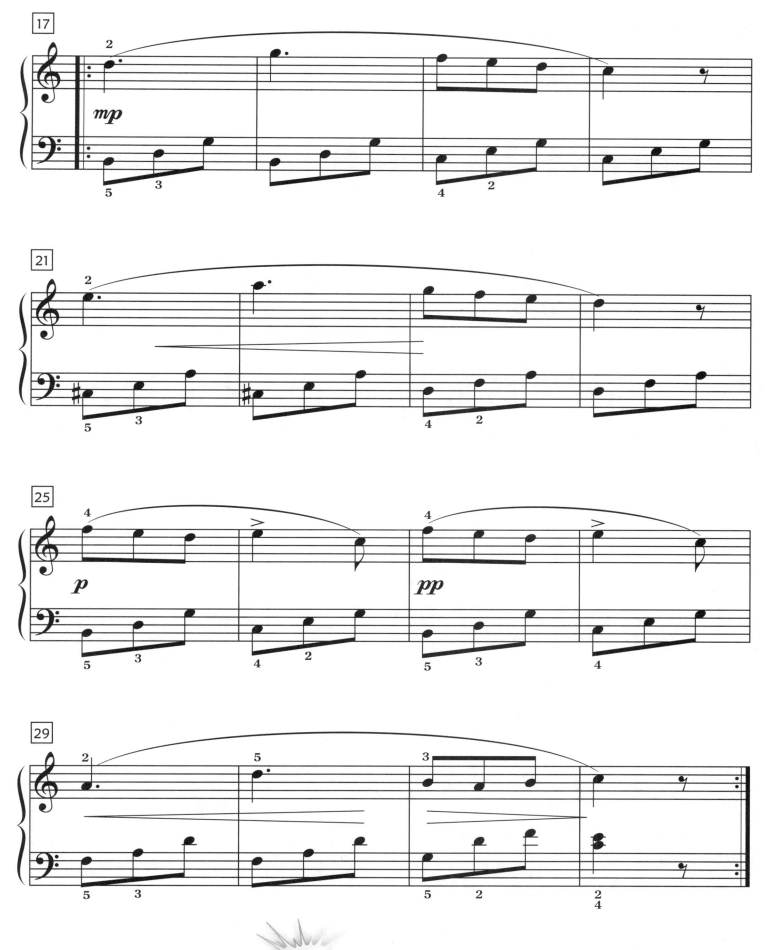

Premier Performer

Let the LH accompaniment flow from measure to measure.

Cloudy Day

CD 31/32

Ludvig Schytte
(1848–1909)

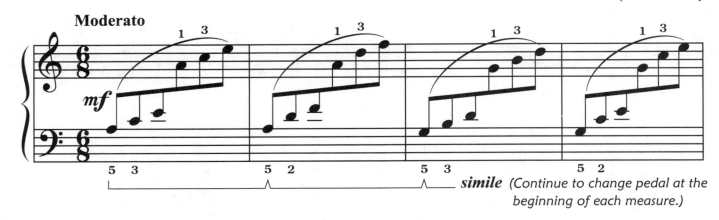

simile (Continue to change pedal at the beginning of each measure.)

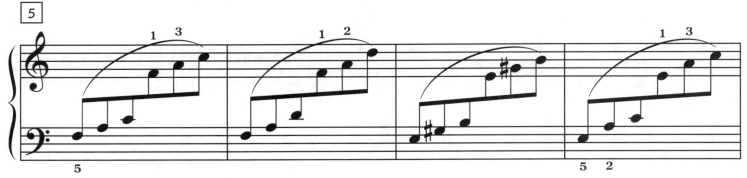

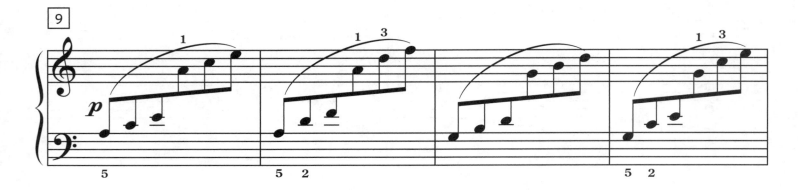

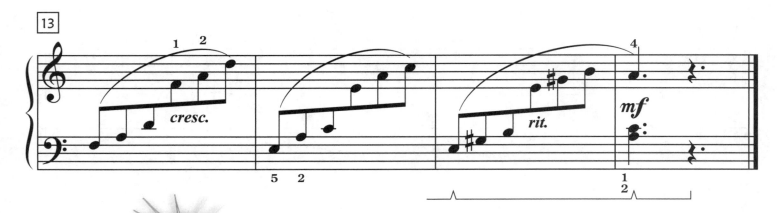

Premier Performer

Let the broken chords flow from hand to hand, sounding like one continuous line in each measure.

Starry Night

CD 33/34

Ludvig Schytte
(1848–1909)

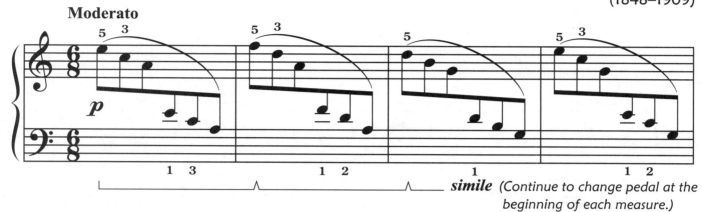

simile (Continue to change pedal at the beginning of each measure.)

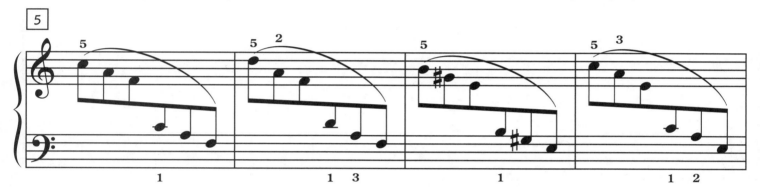

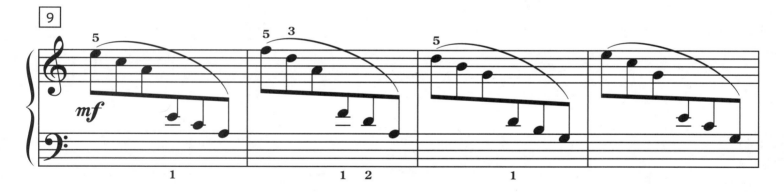

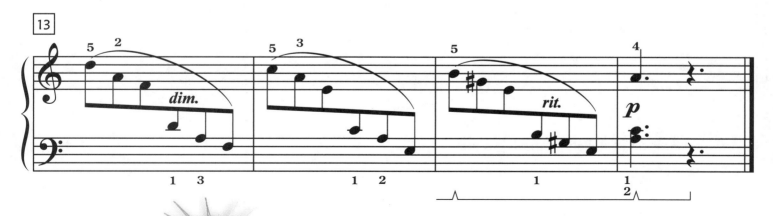

Premier Performer

For a longer performance, play Cloudy Day on page 24 followed by Starry Night without stopping in between.

Lesson Book: pages 38–39

Tarantella* in D Minor

CD 35/36

Alexander Goedicke
(1877–1957)

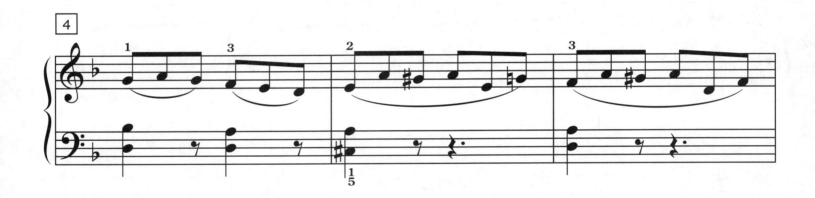

* A *tarantella* is a fast Italian dance in $\frac{6}{8}$ meter.

Premier Performer

Keep the sound smooth and legato when RH 1 passes under or RH 3 crosses over.

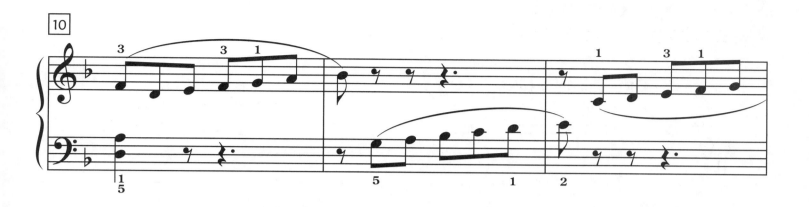

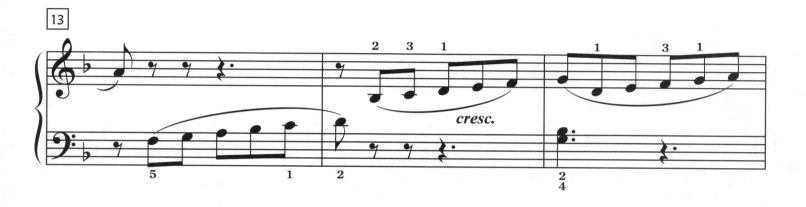

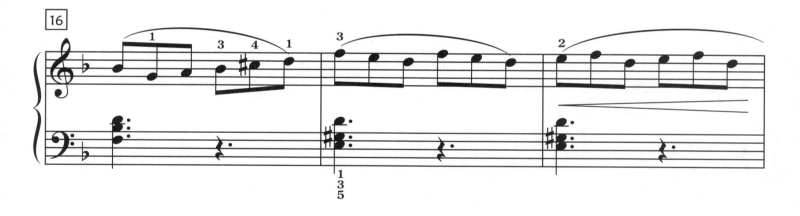

* *sf* *(sforzando)* means "with a strong accent."

Lesson Book: pages 42–43

Spinning Around

CD 37/38

Cornelius Gurlitt
(1820–1901)

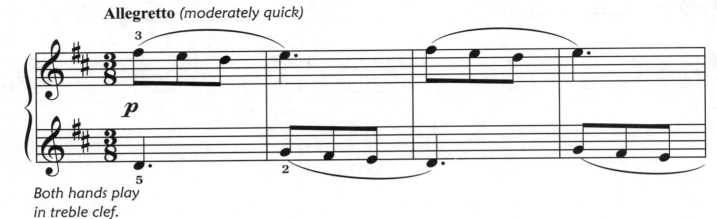

Both hands play
in treble clef.

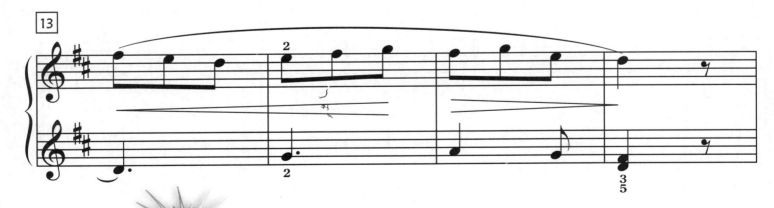

Premier Performer

In measures 1–4 and 9–12, let the LH eighth notes
sound like an echo of the RH eighth notes.

Lesson Book: pages 44–45

The Spinning Wheel

CD 39/40

Ferdinand Beyer (1803–1863)
Op. 101, No. 75

Premier Performer

Shape the eighth note patterns with a crescendo on the ascending patterns and a diminuendo on the descending patterns.

German Dance in D Major

CD 41/42

Franz Joseph Haydn (1732–1809)
Hob. IX:22, No. 2

Allegretto *(moderately quick)*

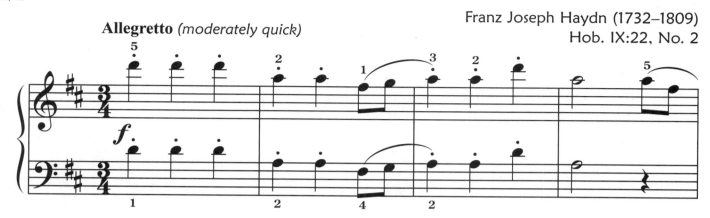

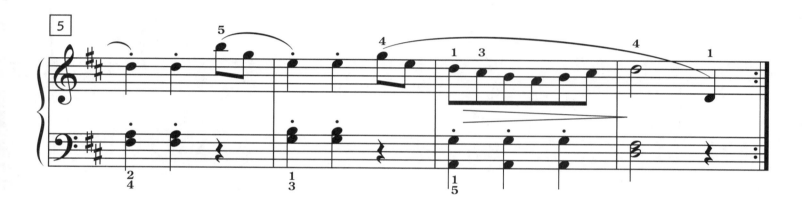

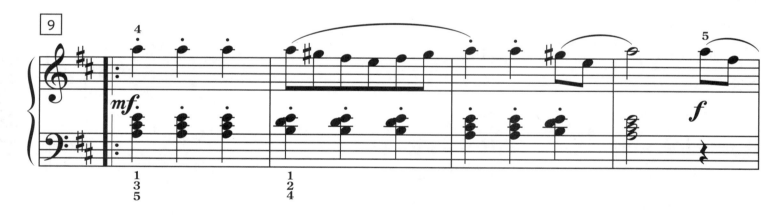

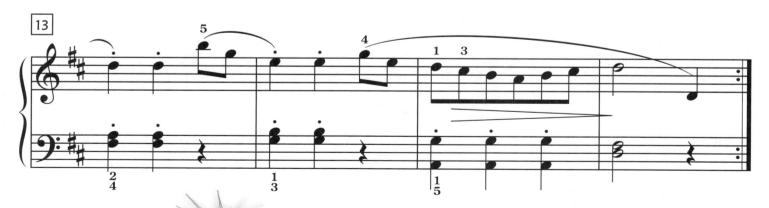

Premier Performer

Move quickly from measure 8 to measure 9 so that the tempo remains steady.

List of Compositions

Note: *Each selection on the CD is performed twice.
The first track number is a performance tempo.
The second track number is a slower practice tempo.*

*The publisher hereby grants the purchaser of this
book permission to download the enclosed CD to
an MP3 or digital player (such as an Apple iPod®)
for personal practice and performance.*

	CD Track	Page
Bagatelle	3/4	4
Bear, The	27/28	20
Celebration Boogie	15/16	10
Chase, The	1/2	2
Cloudy Day	31/32	24
Écossaise in G Major	7/8	6
Folk Dance	25/26	17
German Dance in D Major	41/42	31
Jazzy Trumpets	13/14	9
Little Dance	9/10	7
Opening Act	21/22	15
Setting Sun, The	23/24	16
Soldier's March	5/6	5
Song without Words	17/18	12
Spinning Around	37/38	28
Spinning Wheel, The	39/40	30
Springtime Waltz	19/20	14
Starry Night	33/34	25
Tarantella in D Minor	33/34	26
Trumpet Fanfare	11/12	8
Waltz in C Major	29/30	22

Illustration by Jimmy Holder

CD Performances by Scott Price